Do Something in Your City

Amanda Rondeau

Consulting Editor, Diane Craig, M.A./Reading Specialist

Published by ABDO Publishing Company, 4940 Viking Drive, Edina, Minnesota 55435.

Printed in the United States.

Credits
Edited by: Pam Price
Curriculum Coordinator: Nancy Tuminelly
Cover and Interior Design and Production: Mighty Media
Photo Credits: BananaStock Ltd., Corbis Images, Digital Vision, PhotoDisc, Rubberball Productions, Skjold Photography

Library of Congress Cataloging-in-Publication Data

Rondeau, Amanda, 1974-.
   Do something in your city / Amanda Rondeau.
   p. cm.--(Do something about it!)
   Includes index.
   ISBN 1-59197-571-9
   1. Child volunteers--Juvenile literature. 2. Social action--Juvenile literature. 3. Community development--Juvenile literature. 4. Quality of life--Juvenile literature. I. Title. II. Series.

   HQ784.V64 R663 2004
   361--dc21
                                                          2003058393

SandCastle™ books are created by a professional team of educators, reading specialists, and content developers around five essential components that include phonemic awareness, phonics, vocabulary, text comprehension, and fluency. All books are written, reviewed, and leveled for guided reading, early intervention reading, and Accelerated Reader® programs and designed for use in shared, guided, and independent reading and writing activities to support a balanced approach to literacy instruction.

Let Us Know

After reading the book, SandCastle would like you to tell us your stories about reading. What is your favorite page? Was there something hard that you needed help with? Share the ups and downs of learning to read. We want to hear from you! To get posted on the ABDO Publishing Company Web site, send us e-mail at:

sandcastle@abdopub.com

SandCastle Level: Transitional

38888000170302

You can make a difference in your city by doing something to make it a better place to live.

When you do something to help others, you are making a difference.

Ms. Nealy wants to protect the people in her city.

She became a police officer.

Mrs. Maloy knows many people are hungry.

She works at a food bank.

Mr. Daly worries about dogs in shelters.

He visits an animal shelter and walks the dogs.

Ms. Fife wants to help kids learn.

She became a teacher.

Cindy, Jeff, and Angie want people to be kind to each other.

They put on a puppet show teaching about peace.

James wants to help younger kids learn to read.

He reads stories to other kids at the library.

Gina and Kyle want to make their city look better.

They are helping paint murals in a city park.

Ben thinks flowers help people feel better.

He is planting flowers in pots to take to a nursing home.

There are many ways you can make a difference in your city.

What would you like to do?

Glossary

bank. a supply of goods, such as food or blood, kept for emergency use

city. an area where people live and work that is larger than a town

library. a place that has books, CDs, magazines, newspapers, and other materials that people can use or borrow

mural. art that is painted on a wall or ceiling

nursing home. a place where people who are unable to care for themselves are taken care of

peace. a time when there is no fighting or arguing

police officer. someone whose job it is to maintain peace, enforce laws, and prevent crime

puppet. a doll with a head, arms, and legs that can be moved by attached strings or a hand placed inside it

shelter. a place where people or animals who are hurt or need a home can stay

About SandCastle™

A professional team of educators, reading specialists, and content developers created the SandCastle™ series to support young readers as they develop reading skills and strategies and increase their general knowledge. The SandCastle™ series has four levels that correspond to early literacy development in young children. The levels are provided to help teachers and parents select the appropriate books for young readers.

Emerging Readers
(no flags)

Beginning Readers
(1 flag)

Transitional Readers
(2 flags)

Fluent Readers
(3 flags)

These levels are meant only as a guide. All levels are subject to change.

To see a complete list of SandCastle™ books and other nonfiction titles from ABDO Publishing Company, visit **www.abdopub.com** or contact us at:

4940 Viking Drive, Edina, Minnesota 55435 • 1-800-800-1312 • fax: 1-952-831-1632